One Hundred Things to do at

Before You Die

THE ULTIMATE BUCKET LIST –
UNIVERSAL STUDIOS HOLLYWOOD
EDITION

CATHERINE F. OLEN

One Hundred Things to do at Universal Studios Hollywood Before you Die
The Ultimate Bucket List – Universal Studios Hollywood Edition

© 2020 Catherine Olen

All Rights Reserved. No portion of this book may be reproduced, stored in a retrieval system, or transmitted in any form or by any means – electronic, mechanical, photocopy, recording, scanning or other – except for brief quotations in critical reviews or articles, without the prior written permission of the publisher. Subject to permission under section 107 and/or 108 of the 1976 United States Copyright act. Permission requests should be addressed to the publisher wwww.mousehangover.com. 949-234-7332

First paperback edition August 2020
ISBN 978-1-64822-012-8 (paperback)
ISBN 978-1-64822-013-5 (eBook)

Published by Mouse Hangover
www.Mousehangover.com

Please note: Every effort has been made to ensure the accuracy of the information throughout this book. The information is believed to be accurate at the time of printing. The publish and author are not responsible for errors or omissions for changes to details or the consequences of the reader's reliance on the information provided.
Attraction closures or updates are not the responsibility of the publisher or author and cannot be guaranteed at the time of use of this book.

Readers are welcome to contact the publisher for comments, updates, or questions.

Disclaimer

Several Universal enthusiasts have verified all of the information found in this book, but I am aware that the décor of Universal Studios Hollywood changes regularly. If there are changes, you can visit www.MouseHangover.com for current updates. If you have come across a change before me, please email me so the changes can be noted.

I hope you find your way through the Universal Studios theme park with new eyes and enjoy your hunt for the details every guest can experience.

Note: All content is subject to change without notice. Ride closures, construction, or overlays for the Halloween and Christmas holidays may alter the content temporarily due to park-wide decorations.

This book uses Universal Studios copyrighted characters, registered trademarks, marks, and registered marks of NBC Universal. J.K. Rowling copyrighted characters, registered trademarks, marks, and registered marks. Living Books owned characters, including Dr. Seuss's characters, registered trademarks, marks, and registered marks. Disney owned characters, registered trademarks,

marks, and registered marks. The Simpsons, a registered trademark of 20th Century Fox created by Matt Groening.

All reference to celebrity names, trademarks, marks, and registers marks are the property of the governing body and, Mousehangover.com is in no way affiliated with these entities.

All references to these properties are made solely for editorial purposes. Neither the author nor the publisher makes any commercial claim to their use, and neither is affiliated with Universal Studios or NBC in any way.

About the Author

Catherine Olen has been visiting Universal Studios theme parks since she was a small child. Olen fell in love with the parks built through the imagination of founder Carl Laemmle and became an annual pass holder in 1991 and has held an annual pass ever since.

Olen first traveled to Universal Studios Hollywood at the age of six and immediately fall in love with the Hollywood theme park. She has traveled to the Universal Studios Hollywood theme parks each year since and now visit Universal Studios Hollywood several times a month to revel in the new attractions as well as the classic favorites.

Olen now shares her love of all things Universal in *One Hundred Things to do at Universal Studios Hollywood Before you Die.*

Come Check Us Out

Check out new books, video, and news at
<u>www.Mousehangover.com</u>
Subscribe to Mouse Hangover
Instagram - @TheMouseHangover
Twitter - @Mousehangover
Facebook - @Mousehangover
@WDWScavengerHunt

YouTube – Mouse Hangover

Other books:

One Hundred Things to do at Disneyland Before you Die
One Hundred Things to do at Walt Disney World Before you Die
One Hundred Things to do at Universal Orlando Before you Die
The Great Disneyland Scavenger Hunt
The Great Walt Disney World Scavenger Hunt
The Great Universal Orlando Scavenger Hunt
The Great Universal Studios Hollywood Scavenger Hunt

Dedication

This book is dedicated to everyone who supported me in writing this book.

To everyone who has sat in the darkened theater being transported by the magic of films.

To the dreamers who make their vision reality

To all the movie makers past and present, that bring us joy, excitement, and terror on the silver screen.

And finally, to Carl Laemmle for daring what others fear and creating this amazing movie studio.

Table of Contents

Introduction xi

Before you Enter the Theme Park 1

Upper Lot 8
   Pets Place 16
   Despicable Me: Minion Mayhem 18
   Paris 23
   DreamWorks™ Theater Featuring Kung Fu Panda .. 26

The Wizarding World of Harry Potter™: Hogsmeade™ 30
   Zonko's™ Joke Shop 32
   Honeydukes™ 33
   Three Broomsticks 33
   Ollivanders™ 36
   The Owl Post™ 37
   Dervish and Banges™ 38
   Gladrags Wizardwear™ 39
   Flight of the Hippogriff™ 41
   Harry Potter and the Forbidden Journey™ 42

Springfield: Home of the Simpsons 51
   Moe's Tavern 56
   Duff Brewery 58
   Cletus Chicken Shack 59
   Kwik-E-Mart 62
   The Simpson's Ride 63

Shows	68
WaterWorld®	69
Lower Lot	72
Jurassic World	73
Revenge of the Mummy: The Ride℠	77
Transformers™: The Ride 3D	78
The World-Famous Studio Tour	82
Universal Studios Hollywood Events	103
Conclusion	106

Introduction

Any history of Universal Studios Hollywood must begin with the founder, Carl Laemmle, who worked in the dry good industry until one day in Chicago, Illinois when Laemmle wandered into a nickelodeon and saw his first flicker. While there are no specific records of this part of Laemmle's life, the stories passed down through the years talk about how he stood outside a nickelodeon counting the house receipts for an entire day. Shortly after, he purchased several nickelodeons for himself.

In 1909, Laemmle began his first film making endeavor with the Yankee Film Company with two partners. Laemmle expanded his holdings with the Independent Moving Picture Company in New Jersey.

Word of mouth says that Laemmle changed the face of early film making by crediting screen credits for the actors seen in his films. Other filmmakers kept the identities of their actor's secret so that they could interchange them at will. Laemmle found this would enhance the interest in his films greatly.

The Universal Film Manufacturing Company was incorporated in 1912 with Laemmle and his numerous partners, but Universal Studios, a two-hundred and thirty-acre studio was opened in North Hollywood in 1915.

Almost immediately, the gates of Universal Studios were opened to the public, where, for a mere twenty-five cents, you could watch your favorite celebrities act out the latest film property.

In the early 1920s, Universal acquired character actor Lon Chaney and, with the completion of *The Hunchback of Notre Dame* and *The Phantom of the Opera*, found two of Universal's biggest success to date.

In 1928, Laemmle promoted his son, Carl Jr., to head the studio and the young Carl was able to convince his father to move forward with sound, thus bringing Universal Studios to a new era of filmmaking. One of the first sound films, *All Quiet on the Western Front*, won Universal their very first Academy Award for best picture. Unfortunately for the spectators, this put an end to the use of outdoor sets and required the studios to take production inside sound stages to control the ambient noise.

In the 1930s and 1940s, Universal Studios created a name for themselves with a series of movie monster pictures, including *Frankenstein, Dracula, The Mummy, The Invisible Man, The Wolfman,* and the remake of *The Phantom of the Opera*. While they would go on to have immense success with other genres of film, Universal Studios would be forever dubbed Universal Horror.

Like so many other studios in Hollywood, Universal has their ups and downs but always continue to make movies that kept the audiences coming back for more.

It was not until 1961 that Universal would open its gates once more to the public, allowing them to tour the studio lot on buses. The buses were short-lived, with trams taking over to create less noise on the lot. By 1967,

Universal created the infancy of the theme park with a wild west stunt show accompanying the back-lot tours.

It wasn't until 1976 that Universal Studios would premier an attraction so excited it propelled them into the theme park we know today. The Jaws attraction that is still a part of the back-lot tour created a thrill of coming face to face with Bruce, the shark from the 1974 blockbuster Jaws. Soon, Universal created the ice tunnel seen in *The Six Million Dollar Man*, the collapsing Bridge seen in *The Bionic Woman* and *Battlestar Galactica,* each putting the guests right in the middle of the action. Another part of the excitement of the back-lot tour was the possibility of seeing your favorite stars during their workday.

While Universal Studios has endured as a movie-making empire and a theme park, they are one of the most beloved of Los Angeles experiences.

Before you Enter the Theme Park

- [ ] Grab a bite to eat at the Toothsome Chocolate Emporium and Savory Feast Kitchen

    Step in Toothsome Chocolate Emporium and Savory Feast Kitchen and indulge your sweet tooth. Every chocolate you can imagine can be found within this steampunk shop for you to take home.

    Try the menu devoted to chocolate and decadent shakes and desserts. Take home a box of macarons when you are done satisfying your taste for chocolate.

- [ ] Check out the 5 Towers Stage on the CityWalk™

    This concert venue right on the CityWalk™ will create a concert experience every night. Enjoy modern music and lights that combine to make you want to dance.

Check out the concert for live music and special event throughout the year as 5 Towers Stage offers great music experiences.

☐ Get a picture with King Kong on the CityWalk™

Hanging off the building high above the CityWalk™, you will find the biggest star in Hollywood. King Kong is a great picture opportunity to remember your time at Universal Studios Hollywood.

For the perfect picture, find the brass plaque on the walkway to get the best selfie.

☐ Play in the CityWalk™ fountain

The CityWalk™ fountain is a unique experience that lets guests interact in the water streaming from the walkway. During the day, you can find children playing in the water, but at night, the fountain comes alive with lights to create a dazzling experience.

Be sure to spend some time enjoying this beautiful fountain.

☐ Enjoy a donut from Voodoo Doughnut

Step into this bright pink store to taste your favorite donuts created in a fun new way. Within Voodoo Doughnut, the donut artisans have creatively created classic donut flavors with fun décor and flavors not seen in other shops.

Do not miss a chance to savor the Voodoo Doughnut experience on the CityWalk™.

☐ See a movie at the Universal Cinema AMC at CityWalk Hollywood™

The latest movies can be found at the Universal Studio Hollywood CityWalk™. Relax while you watch the biggest blockbuster films and snack on your favorite theater snacks.

Take some time to enjoy your favorite new movies and relax during your busy day at Universal Studios.

☐ Enjoy dining on the CityWalk™

Guests looking for a great meal can find great food along the CityWalk™. If you are looking for something quick, head to the second floor where you can find great fast-food options.

For guests looking for a sit-down meal, you can find everything from Italian, Mexican, Barbeque, or Sushi along with many other options.

Be sure to explore the CityWalk™ to find your favorite meal and enjoy some rest from a very busy day.

☐ Explore the shops of the CityWalk™

All along the CityWalk™, guests can find the best shops in Hollywood. Check out high-end handbags, sports memorabilia, socks, and much much more.

Everything from local small businesses to your favorite shops from your local malls can be found at the CityWalk™.

☐ Take flight at iFly on the CityWalk™

Guests wanting a once in a lifetime experience when you don your flight suit at iFly. This flight simulator gives you the feeling of flight with your private instructor. For those wanting to watch, the instructors show off their skills for the crowds.

Be sure to try your hand at flight at iFly.

☐ Try a spa experience at Zen Zone

Zen Offer a unique theme park experience when you sit at the oxygen bar and choose the oxygen in your favorite scent. The oxygen bar can give you a lift or relax you as you breathe deeply while relaxing.

Guests can deepen their relaxing experience by stepping into the aqua massage and work the knots out of your sore muscles.

One hundred things to do at Universal Studios Hollywood before you die

☐ Shop at the Universal Studios Store

Guests looking for everything Universal can shop at the Universal Studio Store on the CityWalk™. Walkthrough this enormous store and find Universal logo merchandise along with items from your favorite movies.

Get your souvenirs from Harry Potter, Jurassic Park, Despicable Me, and Kung Fu Panda as you wander the different sections of the store.

Everything from clothing, toys, collectibles, and more can be found within the Universal Studios Store.

☐ Get a picture with the Universal Studios Globe

The iconic logo for Universal Studios is the Universal globe, and now you can pose for a picture with this amazing logo in the courtyard of Universal Studios Hollywood.

Get great photos as the globe spins, and fog billows out from the base for a great memory.

☐ Watch a taping of Access

Join your favorite hosts as you watch them tape Access live in the courtyard of Universal Studios Hollywood. This show tapes with guests on camera in the background each day, so be sure to get there early to watch the taping and maybe see yourself on television.

☐ Get the V.I.P. experience tour

Universal Studios Hollywood offers guests a very exclusive tour as you walk through the courtyard to purchase your tickets. Upgrade to the V.I.P. tour and get your own tour guide for the day. Join others on your tour for a tour of the backlot in a private tour bus and get the opportunity to walk through the sets of famous movies.

At the end of your tour, enjoy a private lunch served in the private dining room. A V.I.P. tour is a great option for guests wanting to see the best of Universal Studios.

☐ Get your picture on the red carpet at the gates of Universal Studios

As guests walk up to the enormous gateway entrance to Universal Studios Hollywood, stop to look down at your feet. Yes, you are the latest celebrity to walk the red carpet.

Take a moment to get a picture of you and your entire group posing on the red carpet by one of the professional photographers or with your camera as you become the star of Universal Studios Hollywood.

One hundred things to do at Universal Studios Hollywood before you die

☐   Get a picture with the neon Universal Studios sign

   To the left of the main entrance of Universal Studios, guests will find one of the most iconic signs seen on television. The neon Universal Studios sign has been seen on many of your favorite television programs throughout the years.

   Now is your turn to pose for pictures with this well-known sign.

Upper Lot

The entrance to Universal Studios Hollywood stands on what is known as the upper lot. Guests will find many of their favorite ride and shows in this area of the theme park. While this is the main section of the theme park, there are two additional levels to Universal Studios. Check out the nod to old Hollywood

☐ Find the statue of director Alfred Hitchcock

> Outside the guest relations building, guests will find a bronze statue dedicated to one of the most famous directors to work in Hollywood. Alfred Hitchcock was best known for his work in the thriller and horror genres of filmmaking with such classic films as *Psycho, The Birds, Rear Window,* and *Vertigo*.
>
> Step up to this bronze bust and read the plaque dedicating this statue to the greatest director ever know in cinematic history.

☐ Pose for a picture with the Universal Studios fountain

   The focal point of the entrance to Universal Studios is the large fountain with the film crew statue above.

   Be sure to get a picture with this imposing fountain with the theme park beyond. This offers guests their first picture spot after entering the theme park and the beginning of the excitement of the day that awaits them.

☐ Check out the nod to old Hollywood

   As guests walk through the entrance area into the theme park, notice the building facades surrounding the walkway. Guests will find the actors hotel and Jack Pearce makeup studio, which offers a nod to the old Hollywood and the great Jack Pearce, who created some of the most iconic movie monsters that made Universal Studios famous.

☐ Find the perfect souvenir in Production Central

   Production Central, at the entrance to Universal Studios Hollywood, offers guests a wide array of souvenirs. Everything from Universal themed merchandise to film and attraction collectibles can be found within this enormous store.

Whether you are looking for clothing, toys, collectibles, or movie-themed items, they can all be found within Production Central.

☐ Find the Carl Laemmle courtyard

Carl Laemmle, the founder of Universal Studios Hollywood, has been immortalized with the Carl Laemmle courtyard near the entrance to Animation Studio Store. This enclosed area offers seating and a quiet place to relax from the busy day.

☐ Grab a bite to eat at Hollywood & Dine

Guests looking for a bite to eat can stop in at Hollywood and Dine for a meal or a delicious funnel cake.

Dine in the outdoor patio where you can enjoy your meal in comfort before continuing with your day in the theme park.

☐ Walk through the Animation Studio Store for your next souvenir

The Animation Studio Store offers guests everything they could want from their favorite Illumination movies. Also, find items from The Simpsons, Scooby-Doo, and Curious George, among many others.

Find items from *Secret Life of Pets, The Grinch, How to Train Your Dragon, Shrek,* and many more.

Everything from clothing to stuffed toys and so much more can be found in this delightful shop.

☐ Get a picture with Hello Kitty™

That adorable kitty Hello Kitty™ is waiting for you outside of her signature shop at the entrance to Universal Studios.

Get ready to pose for the cutest picture anywhere at Universal Studios Hollywood.

☐ Stop in the Hello Kitty™ Store

The famous Hello Kitty™ has her own store at Universal Studios Florida, and now you can get everything you can imagine to take home.

T-shirts, plush toys, handbags, and more can be found within this adorable shop, so be sure to spend some time with Hello Kitty™.

☐ Visit with the New York City police

As guests approach the New York area of the upper lot, they may encounter a police officer on patrol. Stop and have a chat with the New York policeman, and he may give you a warning or praise you during your time in New York.

Get your camera ready to pose for a picture with this great character as you enter the theme park.

☐ Chat with the New Yorkers in the second-story windows

High above the walkway through the New York neighborhood, guests will find some of the locals hanging out in their windows chatting with each other.

From time to time, they will gab with guests passing by. Be sure to stop and chat with the neighbors to find out what they have been up to or their recommendations for your day.

☐ Take pictures with SpongeBob SquarePants™

Guests looking for creative pictures will find SpongeBob SquarePants™ near the Animation Studio Store. Get your camera ready for a creative picture with this well-known sponge.

☐ Meet Patrick, SpongeBob's best friend

Get your camera ready for a picture with Patrick, the adorable sea star. Patrick is waiting to meet you and pose for pictures near the Animation Studio Store on the upper lot.

☐ Check out the center of Universal Studios for special events

The upper lot is a large circular design with a central area with large underground fountains. Guests will find their favorite characters signing autographs and posing for pictures on most days.

During special times like Christmas or Halloween, guests will find this area transformed with mazes for the Halloween Haunt or Whoville for the Grinchmas season.

This area is also used for corporate events or stage performances during the New Year's Eve extravaganza. Be sure to stop in the center of Universal Studios on your next visit.

☐ Get a bite to eat at Universal Tower Snack Bar

For guests looking for a snack on their way into Universal Studios Hollywood, stop at the Universal Tower Snack Bar to get a snack and a drink to take with you as you explore the theme park.

This snack bar has a great variety of treats for every taste, so be sure to check out this walk-up snack bar.

☐ Get a picture with Shaggy, Scooby, and the gang

> During your travels through the upper lot, look out for those crime fighters, Scooby-Doo, Shaggy, Fred, Daphne, and Velma. They are out looking for their next adventure and posing for pictures with guests along the way.
>
> Do not miss this great photo opportunity for your scrapbook.

☐ Get a picture with Betty Boop

> Betty Boop made her film debut in 1932 in the short cartoon, *Any Rags*. While Ms. Boop was a black and white character during her origins, Betty has now taken up residence on the Universal lot. She is now in full color, posing for pictures with her adorable red dress and ebony curls.

☐ Get a picture with Lucy

> Lucy Ricardo has jumped off the television screen and onto the streets of Universal Studios to thrill guests with her flaming red hair and classic polka dot dress. Guests may even find her holding a bottle of Vitametavegamin but do not take a drink, unlike Lucy, in the famous episode *Lucy Does a TV Commercial*.

One hundred things to do at Universal Studios Hollywood before you die

☐ Get a picture with Beetlejuice

> Guests will not need to say his name three-time to manifest this crazy dead guy. Beetlejuice is waiting for gross-out guests when he shows up on the upper lot. Be sure to get a picture before he fades away back to the underworld.

☐ Get a picture with Dracula, Frankenstein, and The Mummy

> The classic movie monsters that made Universal Studios famous are lurking along the upper lot looking for their next victim. You never know where this creepy threesome may turn up, so keep your eyes open, or you may be next.

☐ Get a picture with Woody Woodpecker and the gang

> Take a picture with Woody Woodpecker, Curious George, and Chilly Willy when they come out to play with the guests of Universal Studios Hollywood. Look around the upper lot and find these beloved characters waiting to take pictures and sign autographs.

Pets Place

Step into your favorite animated film, The *Secret Life of Pets,* as you walk along the street and see the neighborhood where Max, Duke, and Gidget live and have their adventures.

Look in the windows of the daycare center and the toy store to see the animated film come to life at Universal Studios Hollywood. Now you can ride the Secret Life of Pets: Off the Leash to become a puppy and go through the city to the adoption event.

☐ Find your new pet at the Pets Shop

> One of the newest shops at Universal Studios Hollywood is the Pets Shop on Pets Place.
>
> Pick out your new puppy and select its new bandana and carrier. This new pet is a great souvenir and an addition to your home.

- [ ] Take home your favorite *Secret Life of Pets* plush at the Pets Store

    Within the Pets Shop, you will find Secret Life of Pets themed merchandise, including T-shirts and toys. Along the walls, you can find all of your favorite characters from the *Secret Life of Pets* films, including Max, Gidget, Snowball, Duke, and many others.

    Step in to find your new favorite pet in the Pets Store.

- [ ] Walk along the shops on Pets Place

    On Pets Place, you can walk along and find some of the storefronts from the animated film. The daycare center has cubbies and artwork from the children in the window. Check out the toys in the window of the toy store and see some of the other businesses that make up this charming street.

- [ ] Ride Secret Life of Pets: Off the Leash

    Join Max, Gidget, Chloe, Duke, Snowball, and all their friends as you become one of the pets in this brand-new attraction. You will be one of the puppies up for adoption as you work your way through the city during your own adventure.

Secret Life of Pets: Off the Leash coming to Universal Studios Hollywood in 2020.

☐ Get a pint at Mulligan's Irish Pub

For those looking for an adult beverage during their day at Universal Studios, stop off at Mulligan's Irish Pub in the London area of the upper lot.

Whether you like a pint of lager or something harder, you will find a cool drink at Mulligan's.

Despicable Me: Minion Mayhem

☐ Get pictures with the Minions

The Minions, those adorable little yellow bad guys are looking for guests to pose for a picture with outside Gru's home at Universal Studios. Be sure to get a picture with Kevin, Dave, and Stuart next time you visit Gru's neighborhood.

☐ Ring the doorbells in Gru's neighborhood

As you walk down the row of houses in Gru's neighborhood, be sure to ring some of the doorbells as you go. You may hear some very familiar voices of your favorite characters from *Despicable Me* answering from behind their front doors.

☐ Walk through Gru's house at Despicable Me: Minion Mayhem

Walk into Gru's home, and you will find a treasure trove of the unusual. Stand in the main room and find the family tree showing all of the oddballs in Gru's family.

Gru's daughters have been hard at work decorating the walls while Gru's childhood artwork shows are displayed to show that his plan to steal the moon was planned from his earliest years.

The rhino chair and iron maiden stand high above while the lion head holds the dog, cat, and mouse within its jaws is displayed above the front door.

Be sure to spend some time exploring this truly unusual house before beginning your minion training.

☐ Go through minion training at Despicable Me Minion Mayhem

Being your minion training with an interview with Gru himself before being transformed into a minion and starting your rigorous training.

Navigate the obstacle course and work together with your other minions as you try to complete the various challenges around you. Be careful, or you may have to help Gru save his girls from certain death before you are through.

Be sure to get your groove on at the dance party as you exit this attraction and see yourself on the big screen.

☐ Meet Gru, Margo, Edith, and Agnes

Gru and his family are waiting to meet you outside Miss Hattie's School for Girls on the street outside Despicable Me: Minion Mayhem.

Stop by and get your picture and autographs with this villain turned good guy and his beautiful daughters.

☐ Find your minion gear at Super Silly Stuff

Once your minion training is complete, you can show off your new status with great souvenirs from Super Silly Stuff. Whether you are looking for clothing, toys, or sweets, Super Silly Stuff has everything a new minion could ask for.

☐ Play carnival games at Super Silly Fun Land

Guests of Super Silly Fun Land can step up and play great carnival games to win adorable prizes.

Aim for the spaceship on Super Silly Space killer to win yourself a fluffy unicorn toy or try your best aim at Minion Mishap. Win adorable toys not found anywhere else in the theme park.

☐ Check out the water park at Super Silly Fun Land

Super Silly Fun Land offers guests a great way to cool off on a hot day.

Stop off at the water park to get soaked with fountains, sprays, and large waterfalls designed to get you as wet as possible. Be sure to bring a change of clothes as you will need something for the rest of your day after your time at the water park is done.

☐ Ride the Silly Swirly Fun Ride

Climb aboard and take off on a silly fun ride for the whole family. This adorable ride gives you a chance to ride a cute bug vehicle while you travel around and round Super Silly Fun Land.

Maneuver your ride up and down for more silly fun.

☐ Get pictures with the minions around Super Silly Fun Land

Scattered throughout Super Silly Fun Land, you will find the Minions. Be sure to get pictures with the minion family inside their silly car. Pose with the minion with his duckie innertube or pose with the minions roasting marshmallows over the volcano.

If you look closely at the holes in the planets, you will notice the minion eyes staring out at you.

Everywhere you look, the minions have taken over Super Silly Fun Land, so be sure to get pictures during your time in this charming area.

☐ Have a snack at Despicable Delights

Get a *Despicable Me* inspired treat at Despicable Delights near Despicable Me: Minion Mayhem.

Try a frozen banana or Freeze Ray smoothie in mango or banana. Try a sweet treat or a banana cotton candy. These treats are the favorite of the minions, and now they can be yours.

☐ See the overlook of the San Fernando Valley

Behind the water park in Super Silly Fun Land, you will find a smoking area with a spectacular view of the backlot of Universal Studios Hollywood and the San Fernando Valley beyond.

Get amazing pictures in this little-known overlook area of Universal Studios Hollywood.

Paris

Walk down the streets of Paris and immerse yourself in the old-world charm of the city. Visit the Moulin Rouge or pose for pictures with the characters walking along the street.

Visit the French courtyard where you can have a quiet moment or get a bite to eat with sandwiches or salads in the small bistro.

☐ Walk down the streets of Paris

Enjoy the charm of Paris without a passport when you walk through the Paris area of Universal Studios Hollywood.

☐ Pose for pictures on the scooters

Parked on Paris Street, you will find two scooters waiting for guests to climb aboard to take great pictures to remember your time in Paris.

- [ ] Pose with the characters in Paris

    As you walk along the Paris area, you will find characters right out of a Paris novel. Find the stilt walkers or the Gendarme interacting with guests and posing for creative pictures on the streets.

    Keep an eye out for these great characters next time you are in the Paris area.

- [ ] Grab a bite to eat at French Street Bistro

    Guests looking for a salad or sandwich can find a refreshing meal at the French Street Bistro on Paris Street.

    Sit inside this small café or at one of the outdoor patios while you enjoy your meal.

    Guests looking for pastries can find their favorite at the French Street Bistro.

- [ ] Grab a burger at Mel's Diner

    Step inside Mel's Diner for a classic burger and fries with a milkshake. Enjoy listening to the rock and roll tunes from the 1950s while you enjoy your meal.

    This nostalgic burger emporium is a great place to eat during your day at Universal Studios Hollywood.

One hundred things to do at Universal Studios Hollywood before you die

☐   Find the Faber College façade

>   Fans of the classic film *Animal House* remember Faber College as the backdrop for this hilarious film.
>
>   If you look above the archway between Mel's Diner and the Palace Café, you will find the sign of Faber College, a wonderful nod to this classic film.

☐   Get a bite to eat at the Palace Cafe Deli & Market

>   Step inside the Palace Café Deli & Market for a sandwich or salad when you need a meal during your busy day.
>
>   For those looking for something a little heartier, grab a rotisserie chicken or turkey leg to keep you going.
>
>   Sit in the al fresco dining area just outside where you can watch the action as you enjoy your meal.

☐   Snack on a Cinnabon

>   Walk up to the Cinnabon snack bar and grab your favorite cinnamon roll to snack on while you walk to your next destination. Choose from the traditional cinnamon roll, pecan bun, or a cup of cinnamon rolls.
>
>   Top your sweet snack off with a cup of coffee or Mocha latte.

DreamWorks™ Theater Featuring Kung Fu Panda

☐ Listen to Pinocchio as he talks in his sleep

As you walk up to the ticket booth by the entrance to the DreamWorks™ Theater, you will find Pinocchio sound asleep. If you listen carefully, you can hear him talking in his sleep about the other attractions throughout Universal Studios Hollywood.

Be sure to listen to this cute character before continuing into the theater.

☐ Find the DreamWorks™ characters in the wrought-iron archway

As you work your way through the outdoor queue, you will pass under an archway with decorative wrought-iron.

If you look very carefully, you may recognize the silhouettes of your favorite DreamWorks™ characters throughout the ornate scrollwork so take a quick glance around as you walk beneath the archway.

☐ Check out the DreamWorks™ awards in the cases of the DreamWorks™ Theater lobby

As you wait to enter the theater, make your way over to the wall-mounted shelves with the many awards given to the DreamWorks™ animators through the years.

The DreamWorks™ team has been busy for decades, and the volume of awards shows how these animated films have captured the hearts of the world.

☐ Watch the DreamWorks™ Theater Presents Kung Fu Panda

Join Po, along with his father Mr. Ping and Master Shi Fu, as they travel to the Emperor's palace to deliver a special package.

Travel along on this harrowing adventure when you sit back and enjoy this 4D experience.

Keep your eyes on the theater walls as the action will encompass the entire theater before your show is through.

☐ Listen for the DreamWorks™ characters saying goodbye

As you exit the DreamWorks™ Theater, you can hear Marty the Zebra, Shrek, Poppy, and many of the

DreamWorks™ characters offering their goodbyes and offering you safe travels on your way.

Listen to them as you exit the theater.

☐ Meet Donkey from *Shrek*

Donkey has set up his travel office next door to the DreamWorks™ Theater, and he is waiting for you.

Step up and chat with Donkey before getting pictures with this famous best friend of Shrek.

☐ Meet the Trolls

Across from the DreamWorks™ Theater, you can meet the adorable Trolls from the movies *Trolls* and *Trolls World Tour*.

Get your picture taken with Poppy or Tiny Diamond so have your camera ready.

☐ Meet Shrek and Fiona

Outside the DreamWorks™ Theater, you will find your favorite ogre and his beautiful bride waiting to meet you.

Get pictures with Shrek and Fiona for your scrapbook of celebrity meet and greets.

☐   Have a meal at Cocina Mexicana

Guests looking for a great Mexican food meal can find their favorite at Cocina Mexicana.

Try a burrito or taco plate and top it off with a margarita while you enjoy your meal in the al fresco dining area nearby.

The Wizarding World of Harry Potter™: Hogsmeade™

As you enter the magical, mystical world of Harry Potter, you will explore the well-known shops and attractions that bring you right to the heart of the Harry Potter™ books. Become a wizard yourself when you don your robes, hold your wand in hand, and transport yourself to a world where anything is possible.

Fly on a broom as you explore Hogwarts™ Castle or meet a Hippogriff on an exciting rollercoaster.

Join Hagrid as you explore the magical creatures that are his best friends. Be sure to visit the wand master at Ollivanders™ to get your new wand before your time in Hogsmeade™ is through.

☐ Get your picture taken at the gates of Hogsmeade™

> The first photo opportunity you have is at the enormous gate at the entrance to Hogsmeade, framing the village of Hogsmeade.

Be sure to pose for pictures with these famous gates with the Hogsmeade™ sign welcoming you to the Wizarding World of Harry Potter™.

☐ Get your picture with the conductor at the Hogwarts Express™

Standing in front of the platform 9¾ is the conductor for the Hogwarts Express™ waiting to take pictures with guests visiting Hogsmeade™.

Step up and have a chat with the conductor and ask him questions about the train and his job; then, get some great pictures before it is time to move on.

☐ Read the train schedule outside Platform 9 ¾

The Hogwarts™ Express timetable is framed on the wall outside Platform 9 ¾ for guests to check.

Stop to see the timetable for this enchanted train while exploring the platform.

☐ Shop at Hogsmeade™ Station

Inside Hogsmeade™ Station, you can find everything you need for a trip on the Hogwarts Express™.

Everything from clothing, stationery, Christmas décor, and more can be found in this little shop adjacent to Platform 9 ¾.

Zonko's™ Joke Shop

☐ Watch the Wizards Chessboard in the window of Zonko's™ Joke Shop

The display for Wizards Chess shows how violent this form of chess can be as the pieces move closer together, and one breaks apart in the battle.

A favorite game of Ron and Harry, this display of Wizards Chess is another great detail from the wizarding world

☐ Visit Zonko's™ Joke Shop

Inside Zonko's™ Joke Shop, you will find the best jokes from the wizarding world. Check out the Extendable Ears to eavesdrop on your friends or U No Poo for your enemies.

These fun gag gifts are familiar to fans of the Harry Potter books but safe for guests wanting to take home a little bit of the Harry Potter™ world.

Be sure to pick up a Pygmy Puff, everyone's favorite pet, to cuddle in different colors.

Honeydukes™

☐ Watch the Eyeball Bonanza in the window of Honeydukes™

The Eyeball Bonanza machine in the window of Honeydukes™ comes to life every few seconds as the skull tips his hat to reveal a raven who plucks his eye out. Watch closely as the eyeball appears in the slot below.

☐ Get something sweet at Honeydukes

Within Honeydukes™, you will find a world of sweets for any taste. The shelves are lined with chocolates in the shape of frogs, cauldrons, and wands, as well as Pink Ice and Sugar Skulls like the ones you have seen in the Harry Potter films.

Inside the case, you will find Pumpkin Pasties and No Melt Ice Cream on the shelves lined with yummy pastries. Be sure to sample your favorites while inside Honeydukes™.

Three Broomsticks

☐ Find the wanted poster for Sirius Black

Outside the Three Broomsticks, you will find the wanted poster for Sirius Black on a signpost. Watch as Black is thrashing around and snarling at the camera.

Heed the warning to approach this wizard with extreme caution as you continue on your way.

☐ Get a bite to eat at the Three Broomsticks

Inside the Three Broomsticks™, you will find wonderful dishes from the UK. Try Fish and Chips, Shepherd's Pie, or Beef Pasties to keep you going on a long day.

For groups looking for a sumptuous meal, try the Feast, a complete meal for four, one of the best food values throughout the theme park.

☐ Look for the shadows in the Three Broomsticks

As you sit inside the Three Broomsticks™ enjoying your meal, you may catch a glimpse of shadows on the walls that quickly fade away. These are shadows of the house-elves working on the second floor, so keep your eyes peeled for this elusive detail.

☐ Visit the Hogs Head™

Step inside this small bar inside Hogsmeade™ for a cold Butterbeer™ or something little harder. Try a specialty ale or pumpkin juice as you enjoy the coolness of the Hogs Head™.

- [ ] Water the hog head behind the bar

    Mounted behind the bar is a large hog's head, which gave this bar its name. Watch as the head moves from side to side and snorts his displeasure then falls silent.

- [ ] Listen to the house-elves on the second floor of the Hogs Head™

    Walk to the base of the stairs to the left of the bar and listen to the activity on the second floor. Upstairs you can hear house elves working hard to keep the rooms clean and care for the weary travelers.

- [ ] Taste a Butterbeer™

    Fans of the Wizarding World of Harry Potter™ now have the chance to drink the signature drink they read about in their favorite Harry Potter books.

    Step up to the cart on the street and order a Butterbeer™; millions of visitors enjoy this butterscotch flavored drink each year, so step up to get yours.

    Take home a souvenir by ordering your Butterbeer™ in a souvenir mug.

- ☐ Visit the conveniences and listen to Moaning Myrtle

  Step inside the conveniences, known as restrooms in the muggle world, and hear the voice of Moaning Myrtle as she converses with you.

  This famous ghost will whine about her day or poke fun as you take care of your business.

Ollivanders™

- ☐ Attend a wand fitting at Ollivanders™

  Every new wizard dream of getting their wand fitting at Ollivanders™, and now you have your chance to be selected by the wand master during the Ollivanders™ wand fitting demonstration.

  The wand master will select a young student and find the perfect wand to fit the newest wizard.

- ☐ Walk through the wand displays at Ollivanders™

  Find your perfect wand at Ollivanders™ after you have finished the wand fitting demonstration. Whether you are looking for the wand of your favorite Harry Potter character or a custom wand of your own, you will find the perfect wand to take home with you.

The shelves are lined with thousands of wands in every shape and color, so take your time to let the perfect wand pick you.

The Owl Post™

☐ Visit the Owl Post

Step inside the Owl Post™ to get all of your stationery needs. Whether you are looking for stationery, quills, stamps, or postcards, you will find everything within the Owl Post™.

Examine the stacks of packages waiting for the owls to deliver to their new owners before looking above at the owls resting before they head out again.

☐ Listen to the Howlers outside the Owl Post

Step outside the owl post and look at the window between the packages. Unexpectedly a howler will appear and yell at you about a variety of infractions. Be sure to spend time watching the howlers to get all of your messages before moving on.

Dervish and Banges™

☐ Find the Monster book of Monsters in Dervish and Banges™

Step into Dervish and Banges and find the Monster Book of Monster sitting in the center of the room in a cage.

This sleeping book may just wake up and try to attack the guests looking, so be careful and do not stick your fingers in the cage.

☐ Find the brooms tethered within Dervish and Banges™

High above the first floor, you will see three brooms tethered to the second-floor rail. Watch them as they sway in the air waiting for their owners to return.

☐ Read the closing instructions in Dervish and Banges™

Behind the counter of Dervish and Banges™, you will find the closing instructions for the staff to follow each evening.

Read the numbered list, and you will see how detailed the closing of this wizarding shop can be for the staff.

- ☐ Find the model of Hogwarts™ in the window of Dervish and Banges™

    Outside Dervish and Banges™, you will find a detailed model of Hogwarts™ castle. If you wave your interactive wand, you can bring the dragon to life to chase the poor Quidditch™ player.

Gladrags Wizardwear™

- ☐ Purchase your own robes in Gladrags Wizardwear™

    New students in Hogwarts™ can step into Gladrags Wizardwear™ and find the perfect size. Within this specialty store, you can also find scarves, ties, and accessories to complete your ensemble.

- ☐ Find the sweater given to Ron and Harry by Mrs. Weasley

    Inside Gladrags Wizardwear™, you will find an item that is not sold anywhere else in Hogsmeade™.

    Gladrags sells the sweater given to Ron and Harry by Mrs. Weasley *in Harry Potter and the Sorcerer's Stone*. These wool sweaters can now be yours to wear on a chilly Christmas morning, just like Ron and Harry.

- [ ] Admire the Yule Ball gowns within Gladrags Wizardwear™

    Fans of the Harry Potter films will recognize the gowns hanging on the mannequins within this shop. Hermione's pink gown can be purchased, but the other gowns are one of a kind and not available for purchase.

- [ ] Find your magical supplies at Wiseacre's Wizarding Equipment

    For new wizards, step into Wiseacre's Wizarding Equipment and find everything you need for the school year.

    Wiseacre's offers a supply of clothing along with time turners, crystal balls, hourglasses, and much more.

- [ ] Get something cold at the Magic Neep™ Cart

    The Magic Neep™ Cart offers guests cold drinks for their travels through Hogsmeade™. At the Magic Neep™ Cart, you will find Gilly Water and Pumpkin Juice, adult beverages, and cold fruit.

    Stop by and get a cold drink as you continue through the village of Hogsmeade™.

☐ Walk through the walkway behind Dervish and Banges™

Through the rear entrance of Dervish and Banges™, guests will find a hidden path that leads behind the building. This walkway is a great option on busy days and gives guests another view of the shops within the village of Hogsmeade™.

Flight of the Hippogriff™

☐ Walk through Hagrid's garden

As you work your way through the queue for Flight of the Hippogriff™, you will come to Hagrid's garden full of ripe pumpkins. Be sure to notice his scarecrow is wearing official Hogwarts's™ robes to scare away pests trying to eat his garden.

☐ Listen to the conversation within Hagrid's hut

As you walk past Hagrid's hut, you will hear a heated conversation within. Eavesdrop on the conversation as you walk by, and you may hear Fang barking also.

☐ Find Hagrid's motorbike outside his hut

Parked outside Hagrid's hut is his favorite motorbike. Hagrid uses this to travel through the wizarding and muggle worlds across the sky.

Fans of the Harry Potter books know this bike was given to Hagrid by Sirius Black, the first owner.

- [ ] Ride Flight of the Hippogriff™

    Step in the ride car and take off on this fun rollercoaster. Wave at the baby Hippogriff™ as you begin your adventure that takes you up hills and down on this rollercoaster fit for the whole family.

Harry Potter and the Forbidden Journey™

- [ ] Walk through the castle at Hogwarts School of Witchcraft and Wizardry

    Enter the dungeon of Hogwarts™, and your journey begins as you work your way through the corridors and into the castle itself.

    Walk the very same halls as your favorite characters in the Harry Potter series of books and keep an eye out for the characters as you will come face to face with them along the way.

- [ ] Find Mr. Weasley's enchanted car

    As you work your way through the outer queue before entering the castle, you will find Mr. Weasley's car parked outside. Listen as the car attempts to come to life again.

Take some very creative pictures with this famous car as you pass by.

☐ Stare into the Mirror of Erised

One of the first things you encounter in the dungeon will be the Mirror of Erised. Fans of the Harry Potter books know this mirror shows the observer their heart's desire.

Keep moving, or you may not be able to look away.

☐ Listen to Neville as he is tutored in the Potions classroom

Neville is busy with extra tutoring in the potion's classroom, and you can stand outside the door of this classroom and eavesdrop on the conversation. If you listen carefully, you will hear him working hard at his studies.

☐ Find the house points within Hogwarts™ castle

As you come through the herbology area and back into the castle, you will find house points for the four houses of Hogwarts™.

It would appear that Gryffindor is currently ahead for the school year.

☐ Examine the statue of the Hogwarts™ architect

> Standing just inside the main entrance to the castle, you will find a golden statue of the architect of Hogwarts™. If you examine the statue carefully, you will find the four mascots of the four houses at his feet.

☐ Find the secret entrance to Head Master Dumbledore's office

> As you work your way through the corridor, you will see a large statue before the corridor curves to the left. This statue hides the entrance to the Head Master's office.

☐ Listen to the paintings that chat with you

> The painting hall of Hogwarts™ has dozens of animated portraits that are excited to greet you and have a chat. Listen carefully to these famous witches and wizards as they may reveal the secrets of Hogwarts™.

☐ Listen to the heads of the houses bicker in their paintings

> The four wizards that make up the founders of Hogwarts™ still cannot seem to get along as they bicker back and forth about the state of the school

and whether muggles should be allowed within the castle walls.

☐ Find the Pensieve within Dumbledore's office

The metal Pensieve sits by the shelves in Dumbledore's office. Fans of the Harry Potter books know this Pensieve is used to see the memories that have been captured when poured out into the water within the basin.

☐ Listen to Professor Dumbledore in his office

As you enter the Head Master's office, you will be greeted by Dumbledore himself. Listen attentively as he gives you a solemn warning about your future and talks about the Defense Against the Dark Arts classroom and the history of Hogwarts™.

☐ Find Harry, Hermione, and Ron in the Defense Against the Dark Arts Classroom

As you enter the dimly lit Defense Against the Dark Arts classroom, you may hear voices without seeing the individuals. Suddenly, you will come face to face with Ron, Hermione, and Harry as they tell you about the school and invite you to watch a Quidditch™ match.

- [ ] Read the blackboard in the Defense Against the Dark Arts classroom

    At the front of the classroom, you will find an old-fashioned blackboard with instructions on how to repel a Dementor.

    Read the instructions as you pass by so you will be able to control these dark figures.

- [ ] Find a secret entrance to the Gryffindor common room

    As you exit the Defense Against the Dark Arts classroom, do not walk too quickly down the hall. The life-size painting sitting quietly in the hall will unexpectedly come to life and cheer for her favorite Quidditch™ team.

- [ ] Listen to the sorting hat

    As you get closer to your ride with Harry Potter, you will find the famous sorting hat. Listen as the hat gives you instructions for the ride you are about to embark on.

    Make sure you are taller than a goblin to ride this attraction.

☐ Ride with Harry and Ron in the Harry Potter and the Forbidden Journey™

Step into your vehicle and let Hermione create the magic to let you fly with Ron and Harry. Keep up with them as you explore the castle landscape before being chased by dangerous creatures and dementors.

Play a game of Quidditch™ before taking a trip to the bowels of the castle. Watch out for Dementors, Dragons, and Spiders as you try to make it back alive.

☐ Explore Filch's Emporium of Confiscated Goods for confiscated student items

Mr. Filch has been busy taking possessions from the Hogwarts™ students, and you can find the boxes labeled with the names of your favorite characters throughout this shop.

Sitting atop the many shelves, you will find nondescript boxes keeping his treasures organized. For other items, he has shoved them into the beams above your head. Within these hollow beams, you will find fireworks, gags, and many other items that will never be returned to their owners.

- [ ] Find Harry Potter's glasses in the confiscated items

    Mr. Filch has been busy taking items away from Hogwarts™ students, and he has taken the glasses belonging to Harry Potter.

    Look in the storage area in the rafters of Filch's Emporium of Confiscated Goods, and you will find these distinctive glasses among the items if you look closely.

- [ ] Find your new Hogwarts™ souvenir within Filch's Emporium of Confiscated Goods

    Everything you could need for a year at Hogwarts™ can be found within Filch's Emporium of Confiscated Goods. Shop by your house colors or pick out your new pet from the various plush pets on the shelves.

    Find detailed collectibles and Christmas items within this shop as you exit the castle.

- [ ] See the Nighttime Lights at Hogwarts™ Castle

    Each evening, after the sun goes down, Hogwarts™ Castle comes to life and lights up the night sky. The castle honors each house and shows the magic of this historic school.

    Be sure to include this stunning visual event during your day at Hogsmeade™.

- ☐ Enjoy the songs of the Frog Choir

    The students of Hogwarts™ take to the stage with their frogs to sing for the guests of Hogsmeade™. Make time to see these talented students in their show on the outdoor stage during your time in the Wizarding World of Harry Potter™.

- ☐ Meet the visiting students at the Triwizard Spirit Rally

    The students from Durmstrang and Beauxbatons are visiting Hogwarts™ to compete in the Triwizard tournament, and you have a chance to see the spirit rally on the outdoor stage in Hogsmeade™.

- ☐ Use your interactive wand throughout Hogsmeade™

    Wizards who purchase the interactive wand can practice their spell casting at various areas around Hogsmeade™. Use the enclosed map to find the areas where you can cast the different spells to make the objects come to life throughout this little village.

    Be sure to get your favorite wand to create a once in a lifetime experience.

☐ Walk through the path straight to Springfield

   Guests exploring Hogsmeade™ will find another walkway that leads from behind Wiseacres and Ollvanders™ straight into Springfield.

   On busy days, this is a welcome area to get to your next destination at Universal Studios Hollywood.

Springfield: Home of the Simpsons

Hang out with your friends, The Simpsons, when you step into Springfield. Explore the games of Krustyland or stop in the Kwik-E-Mart for an ice-cold Squishee. Get a picture with Bart, Lisa, Homer, and Marge or dare to meet Sideshow Bob.

Wind up your day with an ice-cold drink at Moe's Tavern as you immerse yourself in the world of The Simpsons.

☐ Get pictures with the Springfield City Limits sign

Pose for pictures with Lisa, Martin, and Nelson in front of the Springfield City Limits Sign.

Get ready for fun with your favorite family, The Simpsons, as you enter Springfield for cartoon adventures.

☐ Get a donut at Lard Lad Donuts

There is only one donut shop in Springfield, Lard Lad Donuts. The giant Lard Lad stands high above Springfield, beckoning guests to come in and buy the giant donuts, including the class pink donut, the favorite of Homer Simpson.

If you are looking for something cold, try the ice cream at Lard Lad.

☐ Take a picture with Chief Wiggum and his dented police car

Standing outside Lard Lad Donuts is Chief Wiggum, having a donut and cup of coffee. Clearly, he was in a hurry since he crashed his police car into a fire hydrant, and the hydrant is spraying water all over the area.

Take a picture with the Chief before he finishes his donut.

☐ Get ice cream at Phineas Q. Butterfat's Ice Cream Parlor

Step up and get your favorite flavors of ice cream on a warm day.

Whether you want a traditional cone or one of the satisfying sundae's, you will find your new favorite at Phineas Q. Butterfat's Ice Cream Parlor. Try the Big Pink Sundae, including a pink frosted donut, or the Everything but the Kitchen Sink for a taste of everything great at this walk-up ice cream shop.

☐ Eat a Luigi's Pizza

For guests looking for a great Italian meal, look no further than Luigi's Pizza. Step in and try a slice of pizza or filling pasta dish to fill you up during your day.

Sit in the outdoor patio for a relaxing meal and a rest from your busy day at Universal Studios Hollywood.

☐ Grab a hot dog at Suds McDuff's Hot Dogs

The Simpson's dog, Santa's Little Helper, became the mascot for Duff Beer, and now has opened his own hot dog stand in Springfield.

Try Krusty's non-kosher hot dog or Marge Simpson's twisted pretzel with an ice-cold Squishee. This walk-up stand offers great food options to keep you going as you explore Springfield, so step up and check out Suds McDuff's Hot Dogs.

☐ Check out Krusty Burger

Krusty the Clown has opened a Krusty Burger in Springfield, and now you can try the famous Krusty

Burger, the Ribwich, or the Clogger with an ice-cold drink.

Krusty has been busy decorating his new Krusty Burger with his favorite colors and his enormous face high above the ordering counter. Stop in and check out the Krusty Burger next time you are in Springfield.

☐ Read book titles on the doors of Krusty's secret library

The doors to Krusty's library are hidden by bookshelves lined with books with very special titles.

As you read the various titles, you may recognize each book is the title to an episode of *The Simpsons*. The creators have cleverly associated the season and episode number on the spine of each book.

Spend some time finding your favorite episodes.

☐ Go into Krusty's secret library

Krusty has opened his private library to guests of the Krusty Burger, and now you can enjoy your meal surrounded by his art and collectibles.

Spend some time exploring the walls for Krusty's personal accomplishments from his long career and posters from his various shows and charity events.

Enjoy looking through this treasure trove to get to know this famous clown a little bit better.

☐ Find the Gabbo puppet in Krusty's library

Fans of *The Simpsons* remember the episode where Gabbo, the puppet, almost destroys Krusty's careers, but Krusty has gotten the last laugh by hanging the little puppet in his study to show him who the boss is.

Now you can see Gabbo for yourself when you visit Krusty's library.

☐ Explore the artwork on the walls of Krusty's library

Throughout the walls of Krusty's library, you will find drawings and caricatures of the Simpson's and their many guest stars.

Spend some time exploring the walls and see how many of these famous folks you can name.

☐ Find the drive-through window at the Krusty Burger

As you walk on the outside of the Krusty Burger, peek at the side of the building, and you will find the drive-through window manned by one of Krusty's trusted employees.

This cute detail shows that Springfield is a working town within Universal Studios Hollywood.

☐ Check out the businesses in Springfield

As you walk through Springfield, you will find many of the businesses you recognize from the long-running television show.

Look in the window of the Androids Dungeon to see the latest comic books and collectibles or look above for Krusty-Lu studios.

The huge Lard Lad is standing high above the signature donut shop while the Springfield penitentiary is nearby.

Springfield is busy with thriving businesses, and you can see them all during your tour.

Moe's Tavern

☐ Sit at the bar at Moe's Tavern

Moe's Tavern is open and waiting for you to sit at the bar to get a cold drink. Ask the bartender to pour you a cold Duff or a Flaming Moe. Pose for a picture with Barney as he stares into his empty glass or sits at the pool table.

Be sure to look around at the memorabilia around the room or read the bottles behind the bar for some amusement.

☐ Pick up the phone on the bar at Moe's Tavern

At the end of the bar, you will find a bright red phone. Pick up the receiver and listen to Bart Simpson prank call Moe.

Keep picking up the phone and listen to a different joke each time you answer.

☐ Get a picture with Barney from The Simpsons

Barney is standing, waiting for his glass to refill inside Moe's Tavern. While he is distracted, get a picture with this larger than life character during your time inside Moe's Tavern.

☐ Find Sideshow Bob prison escape

If you look up at the Springfield Penitentiary, you will find Sideshow Bob has bent the bars back and is in the middle of escaping by repelling down the side of the building.

☐ Peek in the window of the Springfield Nuclear Power Plant

Peek inside the window of the Springfield Nuclear Power Plant, and you will see where Homer Simpsons works.

His workspace is cluttered with buttons and knobs to protect the citizens of Springfield from a nuclear meltdown, but it appears that Homer is gone for the day.

☐ Press the red button outside the Springfield Power Plant

Near the drums of leaking nuclear goo, you will find a large red button attached to the wall. Feel free to press the button to see what happens.

Will you create a small tremor or a full-scale meltdown of the power plant?

Duff Brewery

☐ Stop at Duff Brewery for a cold drink

Duff Brewery is open and waiting for you to step up to the bar for an ice-cold Duff. This open-air bar offers a great patio while you rest as you sip your Duff or Duff Lite, or a frozen Strawberry Margarita.

Top off your time at Duff Brewery with a sandwich or snack.

☐ Get pictures with the seven Duffs

Standing outside the Duff Brewery, you will find the seven Duffs. Fans of the Simpsons may remember the characters from Duff Gardens, and now they have come to Springfield to pose for pictures with you.

Pick your favorite from Edgy, Dizzy, Tipsy, Surly, Queasy, Sleazy, or Remorseful.

Cletus Chicken Shack

☐ Gets some Chicken Thumbs at Cletus Chicken Shack

Cletus and the Spucklers have opened their restaurant in Springfield, and now you can get their delicious chicken sandwich or Chicken plate. For those looking for the unusual, try the Cletus chicken thumbs with delicious dipping sauce.

☐ Find the Spuckler family portrait

As you order your food, take notice of the large Spuckler family portrait within Cletus Chicken Shack.

You will find Cletus and his wife Brandine with their forty-four children posing for this memorable picture.

☐ Find the Spuckler family long johns

As you wander through Cletus Chicken Shack, you will find many photos and memorabilia of the Spuckler family. Hanging high in the rafters of the restaurant, you will find the red long johns drying after a good washing.

☐ Find the Chicken scarecrow

Hanging on the wall inside Cletus Chicken Shack, you will find the Spuckler family scarecrow.

This chicken-themed scarecrow is cleverly advertising the newest restaurant in Springfield.

☐ Find Spider-pig on the second floor of Cletus Chicken Shack

The famous Spider-pig is hanging out in Cletus Chicken Shack, and you can follow his hoof prints to the second floor to find Spider-pig standing on the ceiling.

Be sure to pose for pictures with this superhero swine at the Cletus Chicken Shack.

☐ Find the Test Kitchen Full 'Er Ups on the second floor

Cletus has been hard at work to create new items for the menu at Cletus Chicken Shack. If you look on the second floor, you will find some of these mouth-watering dishes, including Skunk Puppies and Squirrel Jerky.

Be sure to stop by the test kitchen display to find your new favorite dish.

☐ See the Spuckler Family Band instruments

On the second floor of Cletus Chicken Shack, you can find the Spuckler Family Band musical instruments.

The family has built their own instruments, and now they are on display for guests to marvel in the ingenuity.

☐ Listen for the Chickens on the porch of Cletus Chicken Shack

As you stand on the porch of Cletus Chicken Shack, you will hear the clucking of chickens coming from the coop on the porch.

As you look around, you will find bags of day-old beaks ready for cooking and barrels of a mysterious liquid marked with XXX; it is anyone's guess what is inside.

Kwik-E-Mart

☐ Get a picture with Milhouse in front of the Kwik E Mart

Sitting on the bench outside the Kwik-E-Mart enjoying an ice-cold Squishee sits Milhouse, Bart's best friend. Pose for a picture with this adorable character before it is time for him to go home.

☐ Read the advertisements in the window of the Kwik-E-Mart

The Kwik-E-Mart offers products everyone in Springfield needs, so just look through the window to find just what you need.

Whether it is cat litter, Krusty O's, Chutney Squishees, or diapers, you will find the products everyone uses.

Spend some time reading the packages or signs to get a chuckle before heading in to do your shopping.

☐ Pop into the Kwik-E-Mart for a snack or a souvenir

> Stop in the Kwik-E-Mart to find the perfect gift for that special someone from Springfield. Inside you will find great Simpson's T-shirts, Duff items, toys, or the iconic giant pink donut. Toys for the little ones or pins, including the elusive Bort license plate from Krustyland.

☐ Find the "El Barto" trash can outside the Kwik-E-Mart

> Outside the Kwik-E-Mart, you will find a blue trash can with a spray-painted picture of Homer on the side of it. This is another clever attack from El Barto, the villain tormenting Springfield.

☐ Try your hand at the Simpsons™ Games

> Step right up and try your hand at games of skill at the Simpsons™ Games. Try a dog race, shoot some hoops, throw the baseballs, or whack the rats to win fun Simpsons™ themed prizes you cannot get anywhere else.

The Simpson's Ride

☐ Find Krusty's uvula

> As you walk through the mouth of Krusty the Clown to enter the queue for the Simpson's Ride™, look up

at the roof of Krusty's mouth. You will find Krusty's uvula, the little piece of flesh that hangs above the throat.

☐ Read the advertisements for the attractions at Krustyland

As you work your way through the queue for the Simpson's Ride™, read some of the advertisements for the attractions and shows at Krustyland.

You will recognize some of your favorite Simpson's characters in the shows and rides you will experience at Krustyland.

☐ Watch the clips from the Simpsons while in the queue for the Simpson's Ride

Watch the monitors to see clips from your favorite episodes of the Simpsons. The Simpsons know how to grow your excitement for Krustyland by showing your favorite moments from the past, so enjoy this look back at the Simpsons.

☐ Check out the booths in the pre-show for The Simpson's Ride

As you arrive at the preshow area, look around at the booths surrounding you.

Hans Moleman works the information booth while Patty and Selma work the lost and found. Try some of the theme park food or try the games with Groundkeeper Willie.

☐ Survive a day at Krustyland and stop Sideshow Bob

Step in the ride vehicle and start on this wild ride while you try to survive an attack from Sideshow Bob.

Ride the rollercoaster, join the happy little elves, and see the water show as you run for your life. It is anyone's guess which one of the Simpson's will save you from Sideshow Bob.

☐ Get a snack at the Bumblebee Man Food Truck

Bumblebee Man has his food truck parked in Springfield, waiting for guests to try his signature Mexican food. Try a nacho plate or tacos in many flavors.

Be sure to get your food before Bumblebee Man is needed on the set at channel Ocho.

☐ Get a picture with the Simpsons

The first family of Springfield, The Simpsons, are waiting for you to come and pose for pictures in front of the Kwik-E-Mart. Get ready to meet

Homer, Marge, Bart, and Lisa as they gather for fun with the guests visiting their home town.

Be sure to keep an eye out for the Simpsons next time you are exploring Springfield.

☐ Get a picture with Sideshow Bob

Sideshow Bob has broken out of prison and is waiting to meet you in front of the Springfield DMV.

Decked out in his prison jumpsuit, you can get pictures of this elusive criminal within the Springfield city limits.

☐ Visit the Springfield Department of Motor Vehicles

Look in the window of the Springfield DMV you will find Patty and Selma assisting many of the residents of Springfield waiting in line.

See how many of the people standing in line you can name.

☐ Get a picture with Lou and Eddie

Eddie and Lou, the deputies to Chief Wiggum, are standing outside the Springfield Police Station keeping an eye out for dangerous criminals walking by.

Take a moment to pose for pictures with these brave policemen as you walk by.

☐ Find Snake at the Springfield Police Station

As Ed and Lou are keeping watch outside the police station, Snake is escaping out a second-story window of the police station.

One of the most notorious criminals in Springfield, Snake, may continue tormenting the citizens of Springfield if he is successful in escaping.

Shows

Universal Studios sets themselves apart from other theme parks with the amazing shows that take guests behind the curtain of how the movies are made.

Universal's Animal Actors is one longest-running shows, beginning in 1970, allowing guests to see how the animals are trained to work on screen. Universal would continue adding new shows with a wild west stunt show using working actors to demonstrate the dangerous stunts used in the movies.

Over the years, Universal would bring bigger and better shows with the Miami Vice and the A-Team shows featuring a large water feature to add another elect of exhilaration.

The Castle Theater brought one of the biggest shows with the Conan the Barbarian show, with intense swordplay and a gigantic snake coming up from the stage. The Castle Theater would host the Beetlejuice Graveyard Revue and the Creature from the Black Lagoon show before becoming the new home to the Universal Special Effect show.

Now, Universal offers guests the latest innovations to show guests the most up to date technology used in films.

Be sure to include the Universal Studios Hollywood shows in your day to round out the excitement of this theme park.

WaterWorld®

☐ Explore the WaterWorld® artifacts throughout the Atoll

Your WaterWorld® adventure begins as you work your way through the Atoll to the arena. See how these survivors live on the Atoll with tools, watercraft, and remnants of the fish they live on.

The Atoll itself is a marvel in itself. The survivors have used a variety of scrap metal to build a sturdy structure to enable them not only to live but thrive on the water.

☐ See the WaterWorld® show

Take a seat and watch the reenactment of the film WaterWorld® featuring the best stunt performers in Hollywood today.

The performance begins as you enter the theater and interact with the Atollers, and they engage the guests. Be careful, or some of the Atollers may get you wet or even soaked before you take your seat.

Watch as the Mariner and Helen try to thwart the Deacon and his minions. The battle concludes with spectacular pyrotechnics, but you will have to wait and see who survives this epic battle.

- [ ] Watch Universal's Animal Actors

Join the furriest celebrities you've ever seen as you join the trainers at Universal's Animal Actors.

The show demonstrates the training techniques used to ensure these professional animals interact with the human actors on film and television.

You will not only see cats and dogs but chickens, pigs, monkeys, and owls that you have seen in your favorite movies. The trainers will ask for volunteers to assist in animal training exercises, so be ready to volunteer.

Every seat is a good one at the Universal's Animal Actors show.

☐   See the Special Effect Show

Universal Studios Hollywood is synonymous with inventing many of the special effects used in film and television. Now you can join in with a peek behind the curtain of secrecy on how these effects are used.

Every type of effect, from the classic glass matte and Foley techniques to motion capture, can be seen during this exciting show.

The stunt performers steal the show as they demonstrate how they stage fight scenes and fire effects.

You will not want to miss this high octane show, so be sure to arrive early for great seats.

☐   Volunteer as a performer at the Special Effects Show

For guests who want to become a performer, get to the Special Effects Show early to be selected for one of the segments using the audience members.

Are you a scream queen, a Foley artist, or an astronaut? Whichever you want to be, now is your chance to get up in front of the audience to assist in showing how movie magic is done.

Lower Lot

The Lower Lot of Universal Studios Hollywood has gone through many transformations since the theme park opened in 1964. This area was originally part of the front lot sound stages but soon became part of the studio tour where trams would drop off guests to see a short special effects demonstration sponsored by Kodak™.

The Lower Lot officially became part of the theme park in 1991 when the Starway opened to bring guests down to this area independent of the tram. Soon, the Jurassic Park water ride opened, giving guests a peek into the terror of the dinosaur theme park. Soon, the E.T. Adventure opened, taking guests on the bike to E.T.'s home planet.

As the theme park continued to grow, so did the Lower Lot as they replace the E.T. adventure with the high-speed Revenge of the Mummy indoor roller coaster. Guests would once again be thrilled with the opening of Transformers: The Ride 3D.

Now you can experience the Lower Lot with high-intensity attractions that will keep you coming back.

One hundred things to do at Universal Studios Hollywood before you die

☐ Take a trip down the Starway

The crowning jewel of the Universal Studios Hollywood theme park is the Starway connecting the upper lot with the lower lot. Guests can ride the five-story escalator with platforms between that give spectacular views of the San Fernando Valley.

For those looking for a serious challenge, try climbing the three hundred and forty-five steps for an intense workout.

☐ Get a picture of the San Fernando Valley

As you travel the Starway to the lower lot, you will encounter one of the best views of the San Fernando Valley you will ever see.

In the distance, you will find the Warner Brother™ Studios and the Lakeside Golf Course. Get your camera ready for this amazing view.

Jurassic World

☐ Watch the Jurassic World experts on the monitors

As you work your way through the queue for the Jurassic World attraction, your time will go quickly when you watch the overhead monitors.

The Jurassic World experts give thorough information and interviews to grow your excitement for the ride you are about to experience.

☐ Ride Jurassic World

Climb aboard your boat and get ready for the experience of a lifetime as you survive Jurassic World.

Come face to face with some of the most ferocious creatures ever to live as you float through the various paddocks of this dinosaur theme park.

Keep your wits about you as you approach the cage holding the newest asset, the Indominus Rex, before finishing your ride with a plunge from the top of the building. I hope you survive the most exciting ride of your life.

☐ Get a new dinosaur collectible at Jurassic Outfitters

Step off your Jurassic World ride and step into Jurassic Outfitters, where you will find everything dinosaur-related.

Clothing, plush toys, playsets, and high-end collectibles can be found within Jurassic Outfitters for you to take home to remember your time in Jurassic World.

☐ Let the kids play at DinoPlay

While the thrill-seekers are riding on the Jurassic World attraction, the kids can play among the dinosaurs at DinoPlay. This full interactive play area lets kids climb, slide, dig, and run through a dinosaur dig.

Let the kids interact with the Triceratops while they play in this fun Jurassic Park area.

☐ Experience Raptor Encounter

Guests can get up close and personal with Blue, the Velociraptor the new Jurassic World attraction. Watch as Blue's trainer demonstrates how this dangerous predator can be controlled but beware as Blue could go on the attack at any moment.

Pose for pictures with Blue or the full-size Triceratops to show your friends your dinosaur experience.

Keep an eye out for the handlers showing off the newest dinosaur, a baby velociraptor.

☐ Get a drink at the Isla Nu-Bar

For guests looking for an adult beverage, step up to Isla Nu-Bar and get a drink inspired by the tropics. Try a classic Mai Tai or Pina Colada to cool you off on a warm summer day. For guests looking for something new, try a Bird of Paradise or Ti Peach.

Get your drink in a collector's mug in three different designs with an edible orchid.

- [ ] Get a bite to eat at Jurassic Café

    Guests looking for a good meal and a rest from their day can step into Jurassic Café. Entrees to temp your tastes which include chicken, fish, and traditional burgers with an islands twist. Top off your meal with a sweet treat and a cold drink, then sit in comfort as you enjoy your meal at Jurassic Café.

- [ ] Get a snack at Mummy Eats

    Another food option on the Lower Lot is the Mummy Eats stand at the entrance to the Revenge of the Mummy roller coaster.

    Grab a corn dog or a pretzel to keep you going through your exploration of the Lower Lot.

Revenge of the Mummy: The Ride^{SM}

☐ Dare to reach your hand through the hole in the queue for The Mummy

   As you enter the tomb, you will come to a wall with a hole just big enough to fit your arm in.

   Do you have the courage to reach through to see what happens? Only the bravest will reach through and find out what will happen next.

☐ Touch the Book of the Dead in the queue for Revenge of the Mummy

   As you work your way through the queue, you will see several artifacts buried in the tomb for thousands of years. One of these artifacts is the Book of the Dead, found within a crumbling wall.

   Do you dare to reach out to touch this cursed book or walk by without tempting fate?

☐ Survive a ride on the Mummy Rollercoaster

   Climb aboard your vehicle and begin your journey through the tomb of Imhotep. Watch as the tomb comes to life with thousand-year-old mummies coming to life.

Enter the treasure room guarded by Imhotep before he chants his curse, and you take off on a high-speed journey.

Beware of the Scarab beetles before traveling back to an unknown location in the tomb. Only the luckiest guests will survive.

Transformers™: The Ride 3D

☐ Walkthrough the NEST at Transformers™: The Ride 3D

Your time with the Transformers™ begins as you enter the NEST facility. Enter this top-secret military complex and find where the military has stored the AllSpark, as well as parts of the Decepticons, captured during the battle.

Watch the monitors while working your way through the facility, and you will find out about the mission you are about to embark on. Watch out for Megatron as he is hunting for the Freedom Fighters ready to save the planet.

☐ Ride with the Freedom Fighters on Transformers™ the Ride 3D

Optimus Prime needs your help in saving the city from Megatron and his Decepticons. Hop aboard

EVAC and help keep the AllSpark from the clutches of Megatron while ensuring you and your fellow Freedom Fighters stay alive.

Travel through the city while a battle rages around you. Keep an eye out for the Decepticons as they take on many different forms. At the end of your mission, Optimus Prime will thank you personally for a mission well done.

☐ Find your new Transformers™ gear at Transformers™ Supply Vault

Find the perfect memory of your time with the Transformers™ when you walk into the Transformers™ Supply Vault.

Inside you will find toys, clothing, and high-end collectibles for sale. Be sure to explore the racks and shelves to find just the right souvenir of the Transformers™.

☐ Take a picture with Optimus Prime

Optimus Prime is waiting for guests near the NEST facility to get pictures and chat with his new friends. Be sure to have your camera ready to capture this icon of the Transformers™.

Catherine F. Olen

- [ ] Take a picture with Bumblebee

    Everyone's favorite Transformer™, Bumblebee, is waiting for guests near the NEST facility. Bumblebee offers his song choices to talk to guests as they take pictures with these great characters from the Transformers™ films.

- [ ] Take a picture with Megatron

    The good guys are not the only Transformers™ waiting for guests at Universal Studios, Florida. Megatron is ready to threaten guests and recruit new members of the Decepticons outside the NEST. Keep your guard up as you get pictures with this villain, or you may be his next victim.

- [ ] Find a healthy meal at the Studio Café

    Guests looking for a salad or sandwich can find a refreshing meal at the Studio Café

    Find your favorite sandwich or salad options, then sit at one of the outdoor patios while you enjoy your meal.

- [ ] Enjoy your favorite Chinese food at Panda Express

    Panda Express has come to Universal Studios Hollywood, giving guests their favorite food tastes on the Lower Lot.

Choose from Orange Chicken, Beef with Broccoli with a side of rice, or Chow Mein as you sit in the Al Fresco patio to watch the guests traveling to their next ride.

☐ Get a snack or coffee at Starbucks™

Fans of Starbucks™ can get their favorite beverage and snacks on the Lower Lot.

There are plenty of healthy options to accompany the coffee drinks to take with you as you work your way through the theme park.

☐ Get ice cream at Studio Scoop

Guests looking for a yummy ice cream sundae can step up to Studio Scoop and find their new favorite flavors.

For Strawberry fans, try the Strawberry Serendipity Sundae. For a new taste, try the Chocolate Carmel Delight Sundae or S'more's and More Shake.

There is a cold treat for everyone on the Lower Lot at Studio Scoop.

The World-Famous Studio Tour

Board the trams and get ready for the thrill of seeing a working movie studio. Your tour guide will bring the movies to life as you see the sets from your favorite film and television shows.

Classic sets from the origins of silent films to the most elaborate sets from the latest movies will be seen during your tour.

Experience mind-blowing special effects that immerse you in the action. Before you are through, you will have a new appreciation for the work that goes into creating the movies you love.

☐ Take a picture with Marilyn Monroe

> One of Hollywood's biggest stars is waiting for you at the bottom of the escalator for the World-Famous Studio Tour.

Marilyn Monroe is sitting in her directors' chair with her wardrobe surrounding her, ready to take pictures and sign autographs with the guests.

Be sure to take a moment to meet this glamorous star.

☐ Spend some time reliving your favorite films on the Universal Studios timeline

The Universal Timeline is your first experience on the World-Famous Studios Tour. This timeline shows you the origins of Universal films through the most current blockbusters.

As you work your way down this gentle hill, keep an eye out for your favorite films and films you did not know were produced by Universal Studios.

Another hidden gem on the Universal Timeline is the Universal logo at the top of each movie poster. As you work your way through the films, you will notice the logo changes with the years.

☐ Find Fire Station 51

Universal Studios has its own working fire station, and you will pass right by on your way to the soundstage area.

Fire Station 51 has been named after the classic fire station in the 1970's television series Emergency! to memorialize this classic show to the dedicated firefighting professionals.

☐ Check out soundstage 12

The first and biggest soundstage you will see at Universal Studios Hollywood is Soundstage 12 on the front lot.

This enormous soundstage is one of the first enclosed stages build on the lot at the advent of sound films and has been host to many of the classic films known throughout the world.

The castle from the film *Dracula* starring Bela Lugosi, the Frankenstein laboratory from *Frankenstein* starring Boris Karloff, the senate from *Spartacus* starring Kirk Douglas, are just a few of the hit movies filmed within the soundstage. More recently, the television competition show, *The Voice,* has taken up residency within this cavernous soundstage.

☐ Explore the soundstages on the front lot

The soundstages in the front lot of Universal Studios are where your favorite films and television shows are currently being filmed. Now you can travel the road between these soundstages and perhaps see inside the elephant doors to peek at the latest productions within.

Some of the television shows that have filmed in this area include *The Munsters, The A-Team, Quantum Leap, CSI, Super Store, Magnum PI, and The Good Place.*

If you are one of the lucky guests, you may see the stars of these shows walking from their trailers into the soundstage so keep an eye out while traveling this area.

☐ Find Soundstage 27

This large soundstage seems to be just like other soundstages on the front lot, but this soundstage has one feature not found within the others.

This soundstage houses a large underground tank that allows the productions to film water sequences while enabling them to control the sound and weather elements.

Fans of the film *Evan Almighty* remember the large ark seen with large waves crashing over the side. This was filmed in this soundstage.

☐ See the production bungalows in previous dressing rooms

As your tour continues, you will pass by several small beige buildings to the left of the tram. These production bungalows were once used as dressing rooms for the actors and actresses under contract with Universal Studios.

Some of the celebrities that called this area home were Lucille Ball, Jimmy Stewart, Robert Wagner, and Doris Day.

Since the advent of the production offices, the most powerful producers in Hollywood have used this area for their offices. Ron Howard, Steven Spielberg, and Megan Altram are just a few of the producers that have worked on their projects within this area of the front lot.

☐ Find the silhouette of Alfred Hitchcock

The master of horror, Alfred Hitchcock called Universal Studios his home for many years using office 5195 to create these classic films. After Hitchcock's passing, Universal honored this man by painting his silhouette on the outside of the build and you will find this as your tram passes by.

☐ See the newest Hollywood soundstage on the Universal Studios front lot

The last Soundstage to be built on the Universal Studios front lot can be found just across New York Street. This building offers the latest in technology and was built for the production of *Hairspray Live.*

More recently, the reboot of *Will and Grace* and the reality show *World of Dance* have filmed inside this soundstage.

☐ Cross from the front lot to the back lot

Universal Studios Hollywood may seem like one large studio space but the areas are very different. The front lot and backlot area are divided by an imaginary line and you will pass and experience the areas on your studio tour.

The front lot consists of the soundstages, production offices, and building areas that create the sets for film and television. The backlot houses the outdoor sets used for the exterior scenes.

You cross over to the backlot at the end of the production offices to continue the excitement of your tour.

☐ Find Brownstone Street on the backlot

> Brownstone Street is a small charming area where you will see rows of small dwellings. This area has changed over the years but the structures have remained the same and have been used in some of your favorite films.
>
> McCauley Culkin was seen in this area during the filming of *Home Alone 2: Lost in New York,* Tom Hanks could be seen during the filming of Castaway, and Jennifer Aniston and Jim Carey filmed Bruce Almighty all on this small street.

☐ Spend some time on Courthouse Square

> Courthouse Square may be one of the most recognizable areas of Universal Studios Hollywood and now you can experience this area for yourself.
>
> This area of the backlot was built in 1946 for the film *An Act of Murder* and quickly became a popular filming location for film and television. The classic film *To Kill a Mockingbird* starring Jimmy Stewart created the iconic courthouse scene here in 1962.
>
> It was in 1985 that a young Michael J. Fox becomes the lead in a film that would skyrocket courthouse square into the consciousness of a new generation. *Back to the Future* filmed extensively in this area of the backlot creating the small-town feel in 1955,

1985, and 2015. Now you can recreate memories of your favorite films while visiting courthouse square.

☐ Ride down New York street

Most guests traveling through New York Street do not realize how often they have seen this area in films and television. While this area has been host to many of the classic films you love, the current New York Street has been rebuilt twice since the creation of Universal Studios.

The back lot has suffered several major fires that have destroyed the New York Street sets. The first in 1957, but was quickly rebuilt to its former look. Again in 1990, these sets were destroyed by an arsonist working on the lot.

The last fire to destroy these sets occurred in 2008 when Universal employed director Steven Spielberg to assist in creating the New York Street sets you see today.

☐ Visit Skull Island and King Kong

One of the largest celebrities in Hollywood has taken up residency on the backlot of Universal Studios and now you can meet him in person.

Your tram will enter a large building just beyond New York Street and instantly you will be transported to Skull Islands, the home of King Kong.

Watch as King Kong rescues you from a pack of prehistoric predators. This magnificent ape battles dinosaurs while the spiders attempt to board your tram. The finale will leave you breathless before Kong disappears into the jungle once more.

☐ Find the remnants of the collapsing bridge

Just behind the King Kong attraction, you will see a large bridge crossing a small lake and surrounded by brush. This is the remnants of the collapsing bridge attraction that was used on the tour from 1974 to 2008.

The tram would cross the bridge and the bridge would fall to give the guests a thrill. This bridge has also bee featured in several television shows like *The Bionic Woman* starring Lindsey Wagner, *The Six Million Dollar Man* starring Lee Majors, Quantum Leap starring Scott Bakula, and *The Voyagers* starring Jon Erik Hexum.

☐ Visit some of the picture cars from your favorite films

Your tour will continue down a narrow road where some of the most iconic picture cars ever seen on screen are stored.

On this road, you will find the original Ferrari driven by Tom Selleck in *Magnum PI*. The car driven by character Biff Tannen in the *Back to the Future* film is parked nearby while the cars from the film version of *The Flintstones* are lined up next.

The most exciting part of the picture car area comes when guests see the cars from *The Fast & the Furious* franchise of films. The cars you see parked in this area were driven by some of the most talented stunt drivers in Hollywood.

If you are lucky, you will even see the Gyrosphere from the Jurassic World films. This sphere is still used for filming so may not always be in this area.

☐ See the sets and props from *Jurassic Park*

The narrow road continues to offer up-close excitement as you cross over to Isla Nublar and see the vehicles and props from the *Jurassic Park* films.

These screen used props are instantly recognizable including the cages and mobile lab from *The Lost World: Jurassic Park.* The small boat from *Jurassic Park III* can also be found within this area.

☐ Survive a dinosaur attack

As you revel in the props from the Jurassic Park films, you may not be aware you are being watched. Keep your eyes out for dangerous creatures lurking in the thick underbrush as your tram may be subject to an attack from both sides.

The backlot tour is full of surprises and this area is no different. The animated dinosaurs pop out when you least expect it to douse the guests so watch out.

☐ Watch the weather demonstration in Old Mexico

The area of Old Mexico is one of the oldest on the backlot and it gives guests a great example at the level of detail Universal Studios Hollywood uses in film and television productions.

The weather demonstration shows guests how rain effects are used, as well as thunder and lightning to add to the special effects.

Keep yourself dry as this area has been known to create flash floods.

☐ Relive your favorite films from Old Mexico

The sets in the Old Mexico area of the backlot have been seen in many movies, television shows, and music videos through the years. Now it is your chance to see these sets up close as your tram gives you a great view of the detail used on the facades.

Some of the films to use these sets include *Big Fat Liar, Pirates of the Caribbean, Knight Rider, House, and Nacho Libre*. Fans of Lady Gaga may remember seeing this area in her video for the song Judas. Janet

Jackson also used the Old Mexico sets for the video for her hit single Escapade.

☐ Relive your favorite films from Six Points Texas

The western sets that comprise Six Points Texas are some of the oldest outdoor sets at Universal Studios Hollywood. During the silent era of film, the western sets were built on six streets that met in the middle. This configuration allowed the studio to film six films at the same time.

Over the years, the area has grown and changed, but the essence of the old west remains. Some of the notable films to use this area include *Bill & Ted's Excellent Adventures, The Virginian, The Color Purple, Wagon Train, and Saving Mr. Banks.*

Six Points Texas is used continuously for filming and can be seen in many current productions so keep your eyes out for this familiar area of Universal Studios Hollywood.

☐ Find the underwater tank

The area between New York Street and Six Points Texas houses many sound stages and production buildings but one stands alone. The round underwater tank can be found by the road and it is used to film underwater sequences while the camera and crew remain dry.

Guests have seen this water tank in the film *Dragnet* starring Tom Hanks and Dan Aykroyd, *Ghost Whisperer* starring Jennifer Love Hewitt, and *Ted 2* starring Mark Walberg and Seth McFarlane.

☐ Travel around the pacific ocean

As your tram leaves Six Points Texas, you will see a body of water near the roadway. The area was used as the Pacific Ocean in the television series *McHale's Navy* starring Tim Conway ad Ernest Borgnine.

The area was once part of the tour which included the parting of the red sea and a small lagoon which was used for filming *The Creature from the Black Lagoon* in 1954. Unfortunately, Universal Studios removed this part of the tour and built additional sound stages. The water feature is all that remains of this part of the lot.

☐ Ride through the cobblestone streets of Little Europe

As your tram arrives in the area of the backlot known as Little Europe, you will see facades used in some of the earliest productions. The film *All Quiet on the Western Front* was filmed extensively in Little Europe and won Universal their first Academy Award™.

Fans of the horror genre have seen the Little Europe sets in the classic horror films *Frankenstein, Dracula, The Wolfman,* and *The Hunchback of Notre Dame.*

Over the years, Little Europe has been seen in *The Princess Diaries 2* starring Anne Hathaway and Julie Andrews, and the television show *The Good Place* starring Kristen Bell and Ted Danson.

☐ Relive your favorite horror films in the Court of Miracles

The Court of Miracles is one of the most iconic areas of the Universal Studios Back Lot. This small area has played host to some of the greatest classic films starting with *The Miracle Man* starring the man of a thousand faces, Lon Chaney.

Several classic Universal movie monsters have been seen in the Court of Miracles including Frankenstein, the Wolfman, and The Hunchback of Notre Dame.

More recently, the Court of Miracles has been seen in *The Good Place*.

☐ See the set for the television show *Home and Family*

The Hallmark channel has taken up residency on the Universal Studios backlot with the house set near the Little Europe sets.

This house is used for the show Home and Family where guests can see the hosts interview their favorite celebrities in addition to cooking and home décor demonstrations.

☐ Enter a working soundstage on the San Francisco subway set

> One of the most exciting moments on your tour of the backlot comes when your tram enters a working sound stage. The sound stage you will see is a San Francisco subway station that shows guests the level of detail necessary in filming.
>
> You will see the craft services table and lights along the wall waiting for the crew to resume filming during your tour.
>
> This set has been seen in the television series *Bones* starring Emily Deschanel and David Boreanaz.

☐ Experience the Earthquake attraction

> Within the San Francisco subway sets, you will suddenly feel the tram rocking as the sets begin to crumble around you.
>
> The Earthquake attraction gives guests a demonstration of how an earthquake can be used for filming while giving you the sensation of an earthquake is a safe setting.
>
> Guests will see the attraction reset itself as the tram leaves the sound stage to get ready to thrill another tram load of guests.

☐ See the sets of Denver Street

As your tram working its way up the street, you will see a small western street to the left. These are some of the oldest sets on the backlot known as Denver Street.

Built in 1964 after a fire devastated the lot, the area was rebuilt to its former glory. The train engine you see on this street was used as an attraction when the tram would stop on the tracks and the train would come towards the tram to stop just in time.

Now the area that remains is used for filming in addition to Six Points Texas.

☐ Visit Amity Island and come face to face with *Jaws*

The tram will bring you to a small village near a body of water. Watch as a shark fin rises out of the water as the shark from the blockbuster film *Jaws* continues to terrorize the residents.

Watch as the shark destroys the area around your tram and suddenly rises out of the water to attack the guests. Keep your head about you so you can survive this shark attack.

☐ See the sets of Cabot Cove from *Murder She Wrote*

> Across the water, fans of the 1980's television series *Murder She Wrote* will recognize the small village of Cabot Cove. Author Jessica Fletcher lived in this small town in this widely popular series.
>
> Now, guests can see the small area where the exterior shots were filmed on the Universal Studios backlot.

☐ See the set on Elm Street

> As your tour continues, you will see a small suburban street to the left of the roadway with several houses. These sets comprise Elm Street used for many television shows and films.
>
> Some of the filmings that have taken place on Elm Street include *Laramie, Rawhide, Wagon train, Adam-12, The Hardy Boys,* and *Emergency.*
>
> The area is still used for filming so keep an eye out for your favorite stars working in this area.

☐ See the Chicken Ranch

> Fans of the hit film *The Best Little Whorehouse in Texas* starring Dolly Parton and Burt Reynolds would instantly recognize the chicken ranch from this popular film.

The white house you see has been featured in many films throughout the years including *House of 1,000 Corpses, Beethoven's 5th, CSI,* and *About a Boy.*

The Chicken Ranch is a unique set on the backlot as the house is a practical set allowing for filming on the inside unlike many of the facades used on the lot.

☐ Travel down Colonial Street

Colonial Street has been a staple of the Universal Studios Lot for decades and guests on the tram will have the chance to see their favorite house facades up close.

Some of the famous homes on this street include the home of the Munsters, the sorority from *Animal House*, the home of Connie Swail in the film version of *Dragnet*, the home from *The Burbs* starring Tom Hanks, the home of *Matlock* starring Andy Griffith, and several homes used in films starring Doris Day.

Colonial Street became Wisteria Lane for the television series Desperate Housewives from 2004 through 2012 starring Eva Longoria, Terry Hatcher, Marcia Cross, and Felicity Huffman. The famous homes from this series are instantly recognizable along with the street itself becoming the backdrop for this television show.

☐   See the sets from *How the Grinch Stole Christmas*

> The enchanting village of Whoville is your next stop on the tour. These charming buildings are original sets from the filming of *How the Grinch Stole Christmas* starring Jim Carrey.
>
> The buildings you see are carved from Styrofoam to enable the builders to create the curved edges needed to create the whimsical world of Whoville.

☐   Travel through the Bates Motel and the Psycho house

> Fans of the horror genre will instantly recognize the Bates Motel from the 1960 film *Psycho* starring Anthony Hopkins.
>
> The Psycho house above is the original set with the figure of the mother in the upstairs window. You will pass by these sets to see the detail that remains after many years on the backlot.

☐   Travel through the crash site from *War of the Worlds*

> The plane crash site is one of the largest outdoor sets in cinematic history. The 747 airplane is a retired working plane that was brought to the Universal Studios lot for the remake of *War of the Worlds* starring Tom Cruise.

The plane was disassembled and made to look like a real plane crash with the debris of a neighborhood surrounding the broken plane.

☐ See the worlds biggest backdrop at Falls Lake

Near the plane crash site, you will see the enormous blue screen area known as Falls Lake. This gigantic screen with the pit area in front is used for filming water scenes where the filmmaker needs to have the ability to control the surrounding area.

This set was built in 1986 for the film *Jaws the Revenge* to resemble the waters of the Bahamas. The sets were left on the lot to be used for additional future films.

Some of the films to use this set include *Sully* starring Tom Hanks, *Deep Impact* starring Robert Duvall, *Oh Brother Where Art Thou* starring George Clooney, *National Treasure 2* starring Nicolas Cage, and *Pirates of the Caribbean: At Worlds End* starring Johnny Depp.

☐ See the log cabin set

In the wilderness area of the backlot, you will see a large log cabin set that was built for the 1988 film *The Great Outdoors* starring John Candy and Dan Ackroyd.

Known as a practical set, the log cabin has been seen in *Naked Gun 33 1/3* starring Leslie Nielsen, Desperate Housewives, and *Shooter* starring Mark Walberg.

☐ Help Dom and Lettie keep the witness safe on Fast & Furious Supercharged!

Enter the garage to keep the witness safe from the notorious Owen Shaw. Check out the afterparty before Owen finds you and the chase through the streets of Los Angeles begins.

Get ready for the thrill of your life as Dom, Lettie, and their gang keeps you safe.

Universal Studios Hollywood Events

- [ ] Visit Universal Studios during Halloween Horror Nights

    Prepare yourself to be the victim of your worst nightmares when you walk through the gates of Universal Studios Hollywood for the Halloween Horror Nights.

    Scarers are lurking in the darkness waiting to attack as you wander the darkened streets. Step into your favorite horror films as you enter the terrorizing mazes throughout the theme park and backlot.

    Wherever you go, monsters are waiting for you so get ready to run for your life and try to survive the Halloween Horror Nights.

☐ Celebrate Lunar New Year

> Each year, Universal Studios transforms to celebrate the Lunar New Year with the cast of *Kung Fu Panda*.
>
> Visit the cherry blossom tree and tie your wishes on the tree then visit the cast of *Kung Fu Panda* and get pictures with Po and Tigress.
>
> Watch the dancers perform traditional Lunar New Year performances then learn how to create Chinese characters. Finally, try traditional Chinese fare at Mr. Pings' noodles.

☐ Participate in Running Universal

> Each year, Universal Studios Hollywood holds the Running Universal events giving guests a chance to run the 5k or 10k and get amazing medals for participating in these events.
>
> Each Running, Universal has its own theme so check the website to find your favorite themes.

☐ Visit Universal Studios for Grinchmas

> Each Christmas season, the Grinch and the Whos takes over Universal Studios Hollywood to show off a real Whoville Christmas.

See the enormous Christmas tree and the Whoville businesses giving guests a taste of the Christmas season. Write your Christmas list and get pictures with the Whos as they wander through this enchanted area.

Get your camera ready to take pictures with the Grinch and Max then stay for storytime or the Whos celebration at the tree lighting.

Finish your time by finding your Grinch gear with a new T-shirt, scarf, or souvenir.

Conclusion

In conclusion, I hope you have enjoyed seeing the Universal Studios Hollywood with *One Hundred Things to do at Universal Studios Hollywood Before you Die*. It has been my great pleasure writing this book, and I hope you have found something that has added to your enjoyment during your time in the theme parks.

I look forward to many years of Universal Studios Hollywood growing and changing. These theme parks have been a part of my life since I was a small child, and I look forward to many more.

www.ingramcontent.com/pod-product-compliance
Lightning Source LLC
Chambersburg PA
CBHW071358080526
44587CB00017B/3118